Hilly Cuisine

Hilly Cuisine

MADHU SARUP

Rupa & Co

Published 2003 by

Rupa & Co

7/16, Ansari Road, Daryaganj,
New Delhi 110 003

Sales Centres
Allahabad, Bangalore, Chandigarh, Chennai
Dehradun, Hyderabad, Jaipur, Kathmandu
Kolkata, Ludhiana, Mumbai, Pune

ISBN: 81-291-0042-8

Design, photography & typeset: Supriya Saran

Printed in India by
International Print-O-Pac Ltd.
B 204-206, Okhla Industrial Area Phase-I
New Delhi 110 020

CONTENTS

VEGETARIAN DISHES FROM KASHMIR

NON VEGETARIAN DISHES FROM KASHMIR

Introduction

The states of Himachal and Kashmir are endowed with a rich heritage of exotic cuisines. They share boundaries and have similar geographical features, however there is a marked variance in the cooking styles of the two states. The flavours and spices used are inherently different, even though often the basic thickening ingredient in both cuisines is curd or cream.

Himachal Pradesh produces a variety of vegetables, hence Himachali cuisine essentially offers a medley of delicious vegetarian fare. However due to close proximity, Punjabi flavours have had an influence on the Himachali palate – and since the past decade-and-a-half, there has also been a considerable rise in the number of meat-lovers.

Kashmiris are known to be voracious meat-eaters, however this book also discovers the lesser-known, albeit as delicious vegetarian dishes. Fennel (*saunf*), dried ginger (*sonth*) and asafoetida (*hing*) are the main spices used; *deghi mirch* and Kashmiri *garam masala* being the other essentials. Cooked the traditional way (on the '*dum*'), Kashmiri dishes retain their aromatic flavours.

Most dishes are cooked in mustard oil (which should be first heated, till it smokes and then heat should be lowered before you commence cooking). Most dishes, especially non-vegetarian ones taste better when cooked in clarified butter (*ghee*). Unless mentioned otherwise, every dish caters for four people.

Vegetarian Dishes from Himachal

MADRA

Madra is a common dish in Himachal Pradesh. The main ingredient in the gravy is curd. Madra is the basic gravy used for rajmah, white chana, arbi or rongi. Here it is made with rajmah.

Ingredients

Rajmah 250 gms. – soaked at night and boiled the next day such that no water remains and it is soft.
Curd 200 gms – fresh home made
Fresh cream 100 gms – blended together with the curd
Oil or ghee 100 gms
Turmeric powder $1^1/_2$ tsp
Red chilli powder 1 tsp
Coriander powdered 2 tsp
Powdered *garam masala* $^1/_2$ tsp
Cloves 5 Cinnamon 2
Green cardamom 4 Brown cardamom 2
Coriander leaves for garnishing

Method

- Pour oil in the pan. Put on high heat, till smoked. Lower the heat, add whole *garam masala* and brown for one minute. Add salt to taste along with the other dry *masalas*. Fry for a few seconds.
- Add the beaten mixture of curd and fresh cream and fry till the liquid evaporates. Add 2 tbsp water; cook till the water dries.
- Add the boiled *rajmah* and cook for five minutes.
- Add about 2 *katoris* of water (150 ml) and boil for five minutes on medium heat.
- Garnish with chopped coriander and sprinkle the *garam masala* powder before serving.

BAIGAN with Khus Khus & Aloo

Ingredients

Eggplant/brinjal 300 gms
Potato 200 gms
Ginger 1"
Coriander powder $^1/_2$ tsp
Salt to taste
Cooking oil 6 tbsp.
Onion 1 small (cut into small pieces.)
Turmeric powder 1 tsp
Red chilli powder 1 tsp
Poppy seeds 50 gms (soaked in water for 2-3 hrs and ground to a paste).
Garam masala powder $^1/_2$ tsp

Method

- Peel, wash and cut potato and eggplant into square pieces.
- Fry these vegetables till golden brown. Remove and keep aside.
- In the same oil, fry ginger and onion for 2-3 minutes on low heat. Add the rest of the *masalas* (except the *garam masala*).
- Add the fried vegetables and pour 2-3 tbsp. of water. Cover and simmer on low heat till water evaporates.
- Add the poppy seed paste. Stir, cover with lid and let it cook for 2-3 minutes.
- Garnish with coriander leaves and *garam masala* before serving.

PALDA
of Aloo

Ingredients

Potato 200 gms
(peeled, washed and cut into long pieces)
Mustard oil 50 gms (heated)
Cumin and fenugreek seeds 1 tsp (crushed together)
Coriander powder $1^1/_2$ tsp
Turmeric powder 1 tsp
Red chilli powder $^1/_2$ tsp
Salt to taste
Curd (beaten) 250 gms
Coriander leaves for garnishing

Method

- Pour oil in the pan. When it's hot, add the crushed *masala* along with the powdered ones. Saute till light brown.
- Add potato and fry on medium heat for 2 minutes.
- Pour 2-4 tbsp of water and let it simmer, covered, on low heat till done.
- Add curd and increase the flame. Stir continuously and when it starts boiling, put off the flame.
- Garnish with chopped coriander before serving.

Palda of Aloo

Teli Mash

TELI MASH

Ingredients

Whole black gram (*Mash/urad dal saboot*) 200 gms – (boiled with salt such that no water remains and it has split)
Mustard oil 6 tbsp
Cloves 5-6
Cinnamon 1"
Onion 1 large
Garlic 5-6
Ginger 1"
Coriander powder 1 tsp
Red chilli powder 1 tsp
Turmeric powder $^1/_2$ tsp
Salt to taste
Curd & fresh cream 100 gms (beaten together)
Garam masala powder $^1/_2$ tsp
Clove 2, Brown cardamom 2
Oil to fry.

Method

- Fry the whole *garam masala* in hot oil for 1-2 minutes.
- Fry the onion, garlic and ginger in oil till it is light brown.
- Add the curd and fresh cream mixture and fry for a few minutes.
- Sprinkle the other dry *masalas* and fry for 1-2 minutes.
- Add the boiled *dal* and 4 tbsp of water.
- Cover and cook on low heat. Put a heavy weight on the cover (like a grinding stone). Cook till water evaporates.
- Garnish the dish with chopped coriander and sprinkle *garam masala* powder before serving.

PATOR

Makes a great tea time snack. It is also served with the main meal. Pator is akin to 'patrel' of Gujarat.

Ingredients

Leaves of calocassia (*arbi*) 12 (washed and wiped)
Garlic 10-12 cloves
Ginger 1" (made into a paste with the garlic)
Gram flour 200 gms (made into batter with water as for *pakoras*)
Salt 1 tsp

Method

- Mix the ginger and garlic paste with the batter.
- Make a cut in the centre of the leaf after removing its stem. (The cut should be from where the stem is removed.)
- Apply a little batter on the full leaf. Place one on top of each other, the leaves facing opposite directions till six leaves are put in layers, applying the batter.
- Now fold the layered leaves from the side, applying batter in the middle to make it like a bundle. Tie with a thread, so that it does not disintegrate.
- Make another bundle of the remaining six leaves.
- Steam the bundle for 10-15 minutes on low heat.
- Remove the thread and cut the bundle into slices.
- Fry the slices to golden brown on medium heat and serve hot with sauce or mint chutney.

Note: If steamed in a pressure cooker, then it will take only 5-7 minutes to cook.

SEPU Wadi

Ingredients

Broken black gram (split *urad dal*) 250 gms – (soaked overnight and washed in the morning to get rid of the skin)
Spinach 50 gms (cleaned, washed, boiled & mashed to a paste)
Whole *garam masala* (2 cloves, 1" cinnamon, 2 brown cardamoms)
Fresh cream 50 gms
Curd 50 gms
Turmeric powder 1 tsp
Red chilli powder $^1/_2$ tsp
Coriander powder 1 tsp
Cumin powder $^1/_2$ tsp
Oil for frying

Method

- Add the *garam masala* to *urad dal*, add a little salt and grind it together. The *dal* should not be fully crushed.
- Mould the *dal* paste into a chunk (like that of cottage cheese) and put it gently into plain boiling water; boil for 45 minutes on medium heat.
- After it has been boiled, it can be cut into 2" square pieces.
- Fry the *sepu wadis* on medium heat in oil till light brown.
- In the same oil, add all the *masals* and fry for one minute. Add the spinach and fry for another one minute.
- Add 1 *katori* (150 ml) water. Let the gravy simmer.
- Add the *sepu wadi* in the gravy and let it simmer for another 2-3 minutes. Serve hot.

KADDU Ki Sabzi
(Dry)

Ingredients

Pumpkin (*kaddu*) 500 gms
(pealed, washed and cut into 1" square pieces).
Oil 150 gms
Mango powder 1 tps
Turmeric powder 1 tsp
Coriander powder $1^1/_2$ tsp
Red chilli powder 1 tsp
Salt to taste
Fenugreek seeds $^1/_2$ tsp

Method

- Heat oil, lower the flame and add the fenugreek seeds. Let it brown. Add mango powder. Cook for 1 minute and add the other dry *masalas*.
- Add the pumpkin. Lower the flame, mix well. Cover with a tight lid and cook till it is tender.
- If need be, add a little water.
- Garnish will fresh coriander.
- Serve hot, with *paranthas*.

Spicy KADDU with Gravy

Ingredients

Pumpkin (*kaddu*) 500 gms – (pealed & cut into 1"
square pieces)
Oil 150 gms
Mango powder 1 tsp
Turmeric powder 1 tsp
Coriander powder $1^1/_2$ tsp
Red chilli powder 1 tsp
Salt to taste
Water 200 ml
Onion 1 medium sized
Ginger 1" piece
Garlic 4-6 cloves (ground to a paste)
Fresh coriander leaves for garnishing

Method

- Heat oil. Lower the flame and add the onion paste. Fry on medium heat till it is light brown in colour.
- Add the dry masalas and fry for 1-2 minutes.
- Add the pumpkin, mix well. Cover the utensil with a tight lid. Cook on low heat till the pumpkin is tender.
- Add the water and let it simmer for 2-3 minutes.
- Garnish with coriander.
- Serve hot, with steamed or boiled rice.

ALOO MATAR
Madra

Ingredients

Potato 200 gms (peeled, washed & cut into medium pieces)
Green peas 100 gms (shelled)
Mustard oil 2 tbsp
Curd 250 gms (beaten well)
Turmeric powder $^3/_4$ tsp
Red chilli powder $^3/_4$ tsp
Coriander powder 1 tsp
Cloves 2-3
Cinnamon 1"
Cardamom brown 2 (crushed)
Salt to taste
Coriander leaves for garnishing

Method

- Heat oil and add the whole *garam masala*. Lower heat, add the other *masalas* and fry for 1-2 minutes.
- Add curd and cook on medium heat till the water of the curd evaporates and oil floats on top.
- Add potato and peas and mix in the *masalas*. Cook for 2-3 minutes, stirring slowly.
- Add 250 ml water and cook on medium heat, covering the pan, till the vegetables are tender.
- Let it boil, uncovered, on high heat for 2-3 minutes.
- Remove from fire, take down the utensil and garnish with coriander leaves before serving.

ARHAR Dal Khatta

Ingredients

Arhar dal 200 (soaked in 500 ml water for 1 hour)
Tamarind 25 gms (washed and soaked in 100 ml water)
Fenugreek seeds $1/2$ tsp
Turmeric powder 1 tsp
Red chilli powder 1 tsp
Cumin $1/2$ tsp
Coriander powder $1/2$ tsp
Mustard oil $1\,1/2$ tsp or pure *ghee*

Method

- Boil the *dal* in the water it was soaked. Add salt, red chilli and turmeric powder. Boil on low heat till cooked.
- Mash the tamarind to take out its pulp and strain. Add the pulp to the *dal* and boil again for 2-3 minutes.
- Heat the mustard oil or *ghee* till it smokes. Lower heat and add the fenugreek seeds. When it browns, add powdered cumin and coriander and pour the boiled *dal* into the *ghee* and cover at once so that the fragrance remains in the *dal*.
- Garnish with fresh coriander leaves before serving. Tastes best with boiled rice.

Ghandiali

Ingredients

Large calocassia (*ghandiali/kachaloo*) 500 gms (cut into square pieces)
Spinach 250 gms (boiled and pureed)
Cumin powder 1 tsp
Coriander powder 1 tsp
Asafoetida 1 pinch
Turmeric powder 1 tsp
Red chilli powder $^1/_2$ tsp
Garam masala $^1/_2$ tsp
Green cardamom 2-3 (seeds powdered)
Curd 250 gms
Mustard oil 150 ml

Method

- Deep fry the calocassia on medium heat till light brown.
- Put all the ingredients except curd and spinach in the rest of the oil and fry till oil separates.
- Add the calocassia, fry for 2-3 minutes along with spinach and curd on medium heat.
- Add 200 ml water and put on high heat in a pressure cooker. After one whistle, lower the heat and cook for 4-5 minutes.
- Sprinkle *garam masala* before serving.

Khatta CHANA

Ingredients

White gram (*chana*) 250 gms (soaked overnight)
Mustard oil 150 gms
Onion 3 large (chopped fine) Coriander seeds 1 tsp
Rice 3 tbsp (soaked in warm water for 1-$^1/_2$ hr. and ground to a paste).
Fresh coriander leaves 1 tbsp (chopped fine)
Mango powder 1$^1/_2$ tbsp
Red chilli powder $^1/_2$ tsp
Turmeric powder $^1/_2$ tsp
Salt to taste
Garam masala 1$^1/_2$ tsp
Water 250 ml

Method

- Heat the oil in a pan till it smokes. Lower heat and add coriander seeds.
- Fry onions till golden brown.
- Add all the dry *masalas* except the *garam masala* and the mango powder, fry for 1-2 minutes.
- Add the *chana* and fry for 5 minutes.
- Add about 250 ml water and cook on low heat till the *chana* is soft. Add the mango powder and cook on low heat for 5 minutes.
- Add the rice paste and cook on medium heat till well mixed and the gravy is thick.
- Sprinkle *garam masala* and chopped coriander leaves. Serve hot with *puris*.

Bharwan KARELE Masalewale

Ingredients

Bitter gourd small tender 500 gms
Onion 2 large grated
Chilli powder $^1/_2$ tsp
Coriander powder 1 tsp
Cumin powder 1 tsp
Anis seed powder $^1/_2$ tsp
Turmeric powder $^1/_2$ tsp
Garam masala $^1/_4$ tsp
Tamarind 25 gms (soaked in 4 tbsp warm water for $^1/_2$ hour, mashed into pulp and strained)
Mango powder $^1/_2$ tsp
Cooking oil 4 tbsp

Method

- Wash and scrape the bitter gourd and make a slit in centre right across. Rub them with salt on the surface and inside the slit and leave aside for one hour.
- Rub and squeeze out the juice of bitter gourd and wash thoroughly.

- Boil them in salted water, adding a little tamarind till they are half-cooked. Scoop out the pulp and seeds and keep aside, discarding any brown/hard seeds.
- Heat 2 tbsp oil in a pan and add the grated onion. Fry on medium heat till brown. Then add all the *masalas* and one tbsp water and fry for 1-2 minutes. Add salt to taste.
- Mix the tamarind pulp and the seeds of bitter gourd in the *masala* and fry for another 2 minutes on low heat.
- Now stuff the *masala* equally and secure with thread from all sides.
- Heat 2 tbsp of oil in a pan. Fry the stuffed bitter gourd on medium heat turning them now and then so that they are evenly browned. They will be tender and ready to serve. If by any chance they are not tender, you can sprinkle a little water while frying.
- Serve hot with *paranthas*.

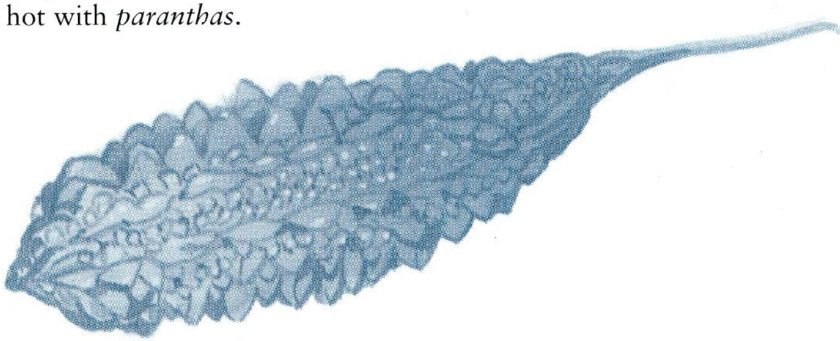

Mixed VEGETABLES

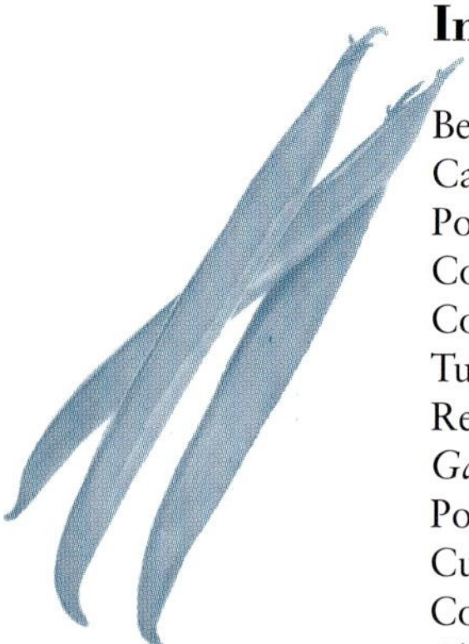

Ingredients

Beans 100 gms
Carrot 100 gms
Cauliflower 200 gms
Capsicums 100 gms
Potato 100 gms
Cottage cheese 200 gms cut into 1" cubes
Cooking oil 3-4 tbsp
Turmeric powder $^1/_2$ tsp
Red chilli powder $^1/_2$ tsp
Garam masala powder $^1/_2$ tsp
Poppy seed 1 tbsp (roasted and ground)
Curd (fresh) 1 cup (beaten)
Coriander leaves 1 tbsp (washed and cleaned)
Cloves 2 crushed
Salt to taste
Brown cardamom 2 crushed
Kasoori methi powder $^1/_4$ tsp

Method

- Boil all the vegetables, which are chopped to the same size.
- Heat oil in a pan. When heated, put the cloves and brown cardamom and fry for 1 minute on medium heat.
- Lower the heat and put all the other *masalas* except the powdered *garam masala* and stir fry for 3-5 minutes.
- Add the beaten curd, mix properly. Put a lid on the pan and cook on low heat till all the vegetables are fully cooked and no liquid remains.
- Serve hot, garnishing with *garam masala* and chopped coriander leaves.

KHEER

Ingredients

Milk 2 litres
Sugar 200 gms
Almond 8-10 (blanched & shredded)
Raisins 15 gms (washed and soaked in warm water)
Green cardamom 1 tsp (powder)
Rice 50 gms (Basmati)
Saffron (few strands soaked in 1 tbsp of warm milk)

Method

- Soak the rice in 100 ml water for $^1/_2$ an hour.
- Boil the rice in the same water till it becomes soft and the water dries up.
- Heat milk in a heavy bottomed pan and add the rice. Simmer on slow fire till it is of creamy consistency. Stir frequently. Scrape out the mixture sticking to the sides and roughly mash the rice.
- Add saffron and the sugar. Cook again on low fire till the mixture becomes thick as it tends to become thin after adding sugar.
- Now add raisins and green cardamom powder.
- Serve in bowls, garnishing with shredded almonds.
- This can be served hot in winter and chilled in summer.

Bharwan Karele Masalewale

Dahi Meat

Non-Vegetarian Dishes from Himachal

Dahi MEAT

Ingredients

Mutton 500 gms
Curd 250 gms (fresh & beaten)
Ginger 1"
Garlic 4-6 cloves
Green chilli 2-4
Onion 2 (ground to a paste)
Coriander leaves 50 gms
Ghee 2 tbsp
Garam masala $^1/_2$ tsp
Salt to taste

Method

- Marinate mutton with curd and $^1/_2$tsp salt for four hours.
- Heat *ghee* in a pan and fry onion paste till golden brown.
- Add the marinated meat and cook on medium heat adding just a sprinkling of water now and then so that the *masala* does not burn. Cook till half done.
- Add the chopped ginger, garlic, green chilli and coriander leaves. Cook on low heat. Cover the pan with a tight lid and add more salt if required.
- Cook on low heat till the meat is cooked and the water dries up.
- Sprinkle *garam masala* just before serving.

Chaach MEAT

Ingredients

Mutton 500 gms
Curd 500 gms
Cinnamon 1" piece (coarsely crushed)
Cloves 2-4
Brown cardamom 2
Onion 2 medium sized
Garlic 4 cloves
Ginger 1" ground to a paste with the garlic
Coriander leaves 1 tbs
Garam masala $1/4$ tsp
Cooking oil or *ghee* 3-4 tbsp
Turmeric, red chilli & coriander powder $1/2$ tsp each
Salt to taste

Method

- Heat a *ghee* in a pan. Put the whole crushed *garam masala*, fry for 1 minutes on medium heat.
- Increase heat and fry the onions till light brown. If need be add a little water.

- Add the mutton and the other ingredients except the powdered *garam masala* and coriander leaves. Fry the meat on medium heat till brown, adding a little water every now and add then till the meat is properly cooked. The pieces should be tender.
- Beat the curd and make *chaach* with 2 *katoris* (150 ml) of water. Add to the meat and let it simmer on medium heat.
- When it forms thickish gravy, the dish is ready.
- Serve hot, sprinkling *garam masala* and chopped coriander leaves before serving.

Vegetarian Dishes from Kashmir

Paneer METHI Chaman

Ingredients

Fresh fenugreek leaves 500 gms (boiled and ground to a thick paste)
Fresh spinach 250 gms
Cottage cheese 500 gms
Mustard oil 200 gms
Cumin (white) 1 tsp
Dry fenugreek powder 4 tsp (boiled in little water and strained)
Salt, turmeric, red chilli, coriander powder to taste
Water (hot) $1^1/_2$ cup
Asafoetida a pinch
Fenugreek seeds $^1/_2$ tsp

Method

- Cut the cottage cheese into square pieces and fry in hot oil till light brown. Remove and keep in hot water.
- Heat oil, add asafoetida. When it smokes add cumin and dry fenugreek seeds and stir for a minute.
- Add the fresh fenugreek leaves and spinach paste and let the mixture cook for five minutes.
- Add the cottage cheese pieces and mix well with the already added, spinach paste. Add salt, turmeric powder, coriander, and red chilli powder according to taste and stir well.
- Pour the water in which the cottage cheese pieces were soaked. Let it cook till the oil floats on top. Serve hot.

Paneer Methi Chaman

Dum Aloo

Nadru MATAR

Ingredients

Lotus stem 250 gms
Shelled peas 500 gms
Mustard oil or pure *ghee* 150 gms
Salt 1 tsp
Coriander powder 1 tsp
Cumin 1 tsp
Anis seed (ground) 1 tsp
Ginger crushed 1 tsp
Dried ginger (sonth) 2 tsp
Sugar 1 tsp
Kashmiri chilli 1 tsp
Asafoetida a pinch
Water 1 cup
A few sprigs of fresh coriander leaves.

Method

- The lotus stem should be thoroughly cleaned. Scrape, wash and cut into diagonal or round pieces as desired.
- Heat oil in a pan and fry the pieces till light brown and $^3/_4$ cooked and keep aside.
- In the same oil put the asafoetida. When it smokes lower the heat and add the ginger, cumin and anis seed and stir.
- Add the peas, salt, coriander powder, chilli powder, *sonth* and stir. Let it simmer on low heat for five minutes.
- Add the lotus stem, stir and add water. Let it cook on medium heat.
- Increase heat to dry up any excess water.
- Serve hot, garnishing with fresh coriander leaves.

Dum ALOO

Ingredients

Small potatoes 500 gms (boiled)
Onions 3 (medium sized)
Tomatoes 2 (finely chopped lengthwise)
Ginger 15 gms finely cut into juliennes
Curd 250 gms (fresh & beaten)
Turmeric powder 1 tsp
Red chilli powder $^1/_2$ tsp
Garam masala (2 brown cardamoms, 2-3 cloves, 1 stick cinnamon 1", black pepper 4-6)
Mustard oil 200 ml
Salt to taste
Coriander leaves a few sprigs chopped fine.

Method

- Fry the boiled potatoes to a golden brown and prick with a fork gently all over.
- Fry chopped onion and tomatoes to form a gravy.
- Add the dry *masalas* and the whole *garam masala*. Form a thick gravy.
- Add $1^1/_2$ cup water and cook on medium heat for 2-3 minutes so that the gravy seeps into the potatoes. See that the potatoes are fully cooked.
- Remove from fire and garnish with coriander leaves before serving.
- Serve with boiled rice or Khamiri Puri.

Spicy Gath Gobhi with Nadru

Ingredients

Knol Knol 250 gms (with leaves)
Lotus stem 250 gms (cleaned & washed throughly)
Fresh coriander leaves 1 tsp (washed and cut fine)
Red chilli powder $^1/_2$ tsp
Coriander seeds crushed 2 tsp
Ginger 2" finely chopped
Garam masala (Kashmiri) $^1/_2$ tsp
Green chillies 2 (cut finely) Salt to taste
Water 200 ml
A pinch of asafoetida

Method

- Cut the cleaned knol knol. Also cut the cleaned lotus stem diagonally into pieces. Prick these pieces with a fork.
- Boil the vegetables till $^3/_4$ cooked.
- Heat oil in a pan till smoking point. Lower the heat and fry the vegetables till they are golden in colour.
- Lower the heat and add chilli powder, crushed coriander seeds, asafoetida and water. Boil on medium heat till the knol knol and lotus stem are tender.
- When about 4 tbsp of water is left, add the ginger and the green chillies. Cook for a couple of minutes on low heat.
- Serve hot garnishing with the *garam masala* and finely chopped coriander leaves.

Kashmiri Puri

The khamir dough

Flour 1 dessert spoon (slightly less than 1 tbsp)
Sugar $^1/_2$ tsp
Curd $^1/_2$ tbsp
This mixture is formed into a dough and left overnight in a warm place. The next morning it is mixed with the following ingredients for the *puri*.

Ingredients

Mustard oil or pure *ghee* 750 ml
Khamir made in the above way
Wheat flour (atta) 150 gms
Refined flour (maida) 50 gms
Salt $^1/_4$ tsp
Sugar 25 gms
Anis seed $^1/_2$ tsp
Milk $^3/_4$ small cup
Water $^3/_4$ small cup
Melted *ghee* $^3/_4$ tbs
Baking powder $^1/_4$ tsp

Method

- Sieve the *atta*, *maida*, baking powder and add the *ghee*, sugar, salt and *khamir*.
- Mix into a dough by gradually adding the mixture of warm water and milk and kneading the dough for about 15 to 20 minutes.
- Add the crushed anis seed and knead for another five minutes.
- Cover and leave the dough in a warm place. In about 2-3 hours it will become double of its original size.
- Divide the dough into 18 to 20 small balls, using a little oil or *ghee*.
- Flatten each ball into a *puri* with a rolling pin rolling on the board by putting a little *ghee* on the board or flattening it on the palm of your hand to about the size of $2^1/_2$ inches in diameter. Flatten and keep aside for 10 minutes.
- Heat oil or *ghee*. Lower the flame to medium heat then fry the *puris* one at a time till they become golden brown. Serve with Gath Gobi and Nadru.

Tasaman

Paneer in gravy of milk & curd

Ingredients

Cottage cheese 250 gms (cut into long pieces)
Cloves 4-6
Brown cardamom 2
Green cardamom 3
Cinnamon stick 2"
Anis seed powder 1tsp
Dry ginger $^{3}/_{4}$ tsp
Milk $^{1}/_{2}$ cup (well beaten)
Thick curd $^{1}/_{2}$ cup (well beaten)
Oil 4 tbsp
Turmeric powder $^{1}/_{2}$ tsp
Garam masala $^{1}/_{2}$ tsp

Method

- Fry the cottage cheese pieces to a golden colour and keep aside.
- In the remaining oil, lower the heat and fry cinnamon and cloves for a minute.
- Add the rest of the *masalas* and salt to taste, frying for a minute or so.
- Add the cottage cheese and $^{1}/_{2}$ *katori* (medium sized) water. Let it boil on medium heat for 2 minutes.
- Add the beaten curd and milk mixture, lower the heat. Cover with a lid and let it simmer for about 5 minutes.
- Serve hot sprinkling the *garam masala*.

Ala YAKHNI

Ingredients

Lauki 500 gms (peeled and cut into $^1/_2$" cubes)
Cloves 4-6
Brown cardamom 2 (lightly crushed)
Asafoetida a pinch
Anis seed powder 1 tsp
Dry ginger (*sonth* powder) $^3/_4$ tsp
Caraway seeds $^1/_2$ tsp
Garam masala $^1/_2$ tsp
Salt to taste
Oil 3 tbsp

Method

- Fry the *lauki* pieces lightly and keep aside.
- In the remaining oil, fry for one minute the brown cardamom and cloves. Add the caraway seeds. Reduce heat.
- Add the *lauki* and the asafoetida. Fry for a minute.
- Add the beaten curd and the rest of the *masalas* and salt to taste. Stir and cover with a tight fitting lid and let it simmer on low heat till the gravy is thick.
- Serve hot.

Phul GOBHI Kashmiri Style

Ingredients

Cauliflower 1 large (600-800 gms) cut into medium sized pieces
Ginger 20 gms (cut into fuliennes)
Cloves 2-3 (crushed)
Brown cardamom 2 (crushed)
Anis seed powder $^{1}/_{2}$ tsp
Degi mirch $^{1}/_{2}$ cup (fresh beaten)
Caraway seeds $^{1}/_{4}$ tsp
Cooking oil 4 tbsp (pure *ghee* preferred)
Salt to taste

Method

- Heat oil in a heavy bottomed pan.
- Fry the cauliflower on medium heat till light brown in colour and remove from the pan.
- In the remaining oil, add the crushed cloves and brown cardamom.Fry for $^{1}/_{2}$ a minute. Remove and keep aside.
- Add the ginger and fry on medium heat till light brown.
- Add the caraway seeds, anis seed, the whole clove, brown cardamom and the cauliflower with salt. Mix and fry on low heat for 1-2 minutes.
- Add the beaten curd and mix well with the cauliflower. Cook on medium heat covering the pan with a lid.
- Cook till the cauliflower is tender. Fry for 1-2 minutes on high flame, till the curd dries up.
- Serve hot, sprinkling *garam masala*.

PHIRNI

Ingredients

Milk 1 litre
Rice (basmati) $^{1}/_{2}$ medium sized *katori* soaked for 3-4 hours. in water
Sugar to taste
Green cardamom 3-4 (seeds powdered)
Almond or pistachio 6-8 (chopped very fine)
Saffron (few strands soaked in warm milk)
Fresh pink rose petals (optional)

Method

- Grind the soaked rice on the grinding stone or mixer to a slightly thick paste adding a little water if needed.
- Boil milk in a heavy bottomed pan.
- Add the ground rice to the milk. Reduce flame and keep stirring till it thickens like a custard.
- Add the sugar, green cardamom powder and the saffron, boil on low flame for one minute. Remove.
- Pour in small bowls. Decorate with pistachio or almond and 2-3 fresh rose petals.

Kashmiri Puri

Rogan Josh

Non-Vegetarian Dishes from Kashmir

Kashmiri Mutton with Khus Khus

Ingredients

Mutton 1 kg (boneless, marinated in curd & salt for 3-4 hours)
Fresh beaten curd 500 gms
Onion 250 gms (grated)
Red chilli powder 1 tbsp
Poppy seed 2 tbsp
Walnuts 50 gms (kernels only)
Saffron few strands soaked in 1 tbsp warm milk.
Green cardamom 3-4 (seeds powdered)
Ghee 150 gms

Method

- Boil the grated onions in a pan for 10-15 minutes in a little water till soft.
- Add *ghee* and the marinated meat.
- Cook on low fire, cover the pan with a tight lid, till the meat is tender.
- Add all the other ingredients and more salt if necessary.
- Once meat is cooked, increase the flame and brown the meat in *ghee*.
- Serve hot.

Kashmiri Koftas
(Rishta)

Ingredients

Meat of lamb 500 gms (minced very fine)
Green chilli 2 (ground to a paste)
Ginger paste $^3/_4$ tsp
Caraway seeds 1 tsp
Red chilli powder 1 tsp
Dried coriander seeds 2 tsp
Brown cardamom (seeds only) 6 crushed
A pinch of asafoetida
Curd 2 tbsp (thick)
Kashmiri *garam masala* $^1/_2$ tsp
Ghee 2 tbsp

Method

- Add the curd, green chilli and ginger paste, asafoetida, brown cardamom (crushed seeds), coriander seeds (crushed), caraway seeds, red chilli powder, $^1/_2$ tsp, salt to taste and $^1/_4$ tsp of *garam masala* to the mince and mix thoroughly.
- Make 20 equal sausage-shaped *koftas*.
- Add *ghee* to a pan and let it melt. When the *ghee* melts, place the *koftas* in it gently. Cover and cook gently on medium heat.
- Shake the pan gently every now and then. Take care that the *koftas* do not break.

- When they become brown in colour, add $^1/_2$ tsp of red chilli powder. Reduce the heat to minimum and cook for another 2-3 minutes.
- Add the rest of the crushed coriander seeds and about 150 ml of hot water and salt to taste. Let it simmer on medium heat till the koftas are tender and the water dries up.
- Serve hot with *chappatis* or boiled rice garnishing with chopped coriander leaves and the rest of the *garam masala*.

Machhli Dum

Ingredients

Fish (Singhara or Surmai) 1 kg (preferably boneless, cleaned and washed)
Fresh curd 150 gms (beaten)
Turmeric powder 1 tsp
Kashmiri chilli powder 1 tsp
Dried ginger powder 1 tsp
Salt 2 tsp
Coriander powder 1 tsp
Garam masala 1 tsp
A pinch of asafoetida (dissolved in $^{1}/_{2}$ cup of hot water)
Mustard oil for frying 4 tbsp
Ghee 200 gms

Method

- Marinate the fish in a mixture of 1 tsp of salt, $^{1}/_{2}$ tsp of turmeric and $^{1}/_{2}$ tsp of dried ginger powder for about an hour.
- Heat oil in a pan, when it smokes, lower heat and fry the fish pieces, two at a time, keep aside.
- Heat the *ghee* in a pan and add the curd and the rest of the dry *masala* except the *garam masala* and let it cook on medium heat.
- When the mixture dries and the *masala* starts sticking to the bottom of the pan, pour the asafoetida water.
- Add the fish to the gravy and let it cook on low heat till the water evaporates and the oil surfaces on the top.
- Garnish with fresh coriander leaves and sprinkle *garam masala* before serving.

Kabargah

Ingredients

Lamb chops 1 kg (ribs, fat-trimmed)
Milk 1 kg
Curd 200 gms
Gram flour 150 gms
Mustard oil 300 gms
Anis seed powder 3 tsp
Coriander powder 1 tsp
Cloves 4-5
Cinnamon stick broken into 4 pieces
Black cardamoms 4
Salt and chilli powder to taste

Method

- Wash, trim and clean the chops.
- Put into the cooker with milk and the spices (tied in a muslin cloth). Let it be on high heat. When the cooker has reached full pressure, lower the heat and let it cook for 15 minutes.
- Remove the chops from the milk and discard the spices tied in the muslin cloth.
- Beat the curd, add gram flour to form a thick creamy batter. Add the other dry *masalas*.
- Coat the pieces of meat with the batter and fry one by one in well-heated, but lowered heat.
- Garnish with coriander leaves.

Note: If any milk remains after boiling the meat, it can be used to cook rice or served as soup.

Yakhni Pulao

Yakhni is the well-simmered stock of meat.

To make Yakhni

Mutton 350 gms (preferably boneless)
Bay leaves 2
Pepper corns (whole) 6-8
Onion (chopped) large
Salt 1tsp
Water 700 ml

The above ingredients should be boiled in a pan with a tight fitting lid on low heat for about an hour or so till the meat is $^3/_4$ cooked. The stock should be about 600 ml. If it is less then add water, strain and keep aside.

Ingredients for the Pulao

Rice (Basmati) 250 gms (soak the rice in water for $^1/_2$ hr.)
Ghee 120 gms
Onions 2 medium sized
Cloves 3-4
Cinnamon 2"
Pepper corns 6-8 danas
Green cardamom 4
Caraway seeds 1 tsp
Poppy seed 1 tsp
Red chilli powder $^1/_2$ tsp
Garlic 6 cloves, chopped fine
Ginger 20 gms cut into thin long slices
Garam masala powder $^1/_2$ tsp
Cashewnuts 10
Eggs 2 (hard boiled)
Mint a few fresh sprigs
Curd 125 gms

Method

- Separate the meat from the bones if there are any.
- Heat *ghee*. Fry the cashewnuts to a golden colour. Remove from *ghee* and keep aside. Fry one sliced onion to a golden brown and keep aside.
- Brown the mutton, take it out from *ghee* and keep aside.
- Chop the other onion and garlic finely.
- Fry the onion, garlic and cloves on medium heat and add poppy seed, cinnamon, pepper corns, ginger and garlic and fry for 2 minutes.
- Now add the meat, caraway seeds, *garam masala*, curd, rice and the *yakhni*.
- Cook the rice in the pan on medium heat. When the water reduces to half, reduce heat and cook on low heat till all the water dries up. Remove from fire.
- Place burning charcoal on the lid of pan, till required.
- Slice the boiled eggs. Garnish the rice with the eggs, cashewnuts and the fried onions. Serve hot.

Shami Kebabs

Ingredients

Minced mutton 500 gms
Broken gram (*chana dal*) 1/2 medium sized *katori*
Garlic 6-8 cloves Ginger 30 gms
Brown Cardamom 2-3 (seeds)
Pepper corn (whole) 1/2 tsp
Garam masala 1/2 tsp Cloves 4-6
Cinnamon 2"
Mint a few sprigs
Salt to taste
Egg 1
Onion medium sized 2 (1 chopped very fine & 1 chopped to fine rings) Green chilli 2 chopped medium sized
Oil for frying 250 ml

Method

- Cook the mince and *chana dal*, adding salt to taste alongwith all the ingredients except onion, mint leaves, green chilli, *garam masala* powder and egg. Cook till done and all the water is absorbed. You can cook in pressure cooker too. After the cooker has reached the full pressure, lower the heat and cook for 15 minutes.
- Grind the mince and add finely chopped onion, mint, green chillies.
- Knead well and add the beaten egg to it, mix again.
- Divide the mixture into 24-30 equal parts. Flatten into round kebabs and deep fry in the oil to a golden brown colour.
- Serve with onion rings and mint chutney.

Dum Murg

Chicken cooked in steam over low heat. This method enhances the taste and flavour

Ingredients

Chicken 1 kg (cut into medium sized pieces)
Dry ginger (sonth) $^3/_4$ tsp
Red chilli powder $1^1/_2$ tsp
Ghee 200 gms
Green cardamom crushed 2-4
Curd 200 gms
Coriander seeds 1 tsp
Whole pepper corns 1 tsp
Cinnamon 1"
Cloves 6

Method

- Marinate chicken pieces with curd, and all other spices in a pan for around $2^1/_2$ hrs.
- Heat the *ghee* in a thick bottomed pan on moderate heat and add the crushed *masalas*. Fry for 1-2 minutes.
- Add the marinated chicken alongwith the marinade and cook for about 15 minutes on low heat stirring all the time.
- Put the griddle on the fire and place the pan on the griddle.
- Make a long roll of the dough and seal the lid on the pan.
- Let the chicken cook on *dum* (steam) for about an hour (less if it is a broiler).
- Break the seal of the pan. Serve hot, sprinkling the *garam masala* powder.

Seekh Kebabs

Ingredients

Minced mutton 500 gms
Ginger and garlic paste $1^1/_2$ tsp each
Red chilli powder $^3/_4$ tsp
Caraway seeds $^1/_2$ tsp
Poppy seeds 1 tsp
Anis seed powder 1 tsp
Brown Cardamom 2-3 (seeds powdered)
Cornflour 2 tbsp or *besan* (roasted)
Garam masala $^1/_2$ tsp
Oil for brushing 2-4 tbsp
Curd 1 tbsp
Steel skewers 6
Chopped coriander leaves 1 tbsp

Salad to be served with the seekh kebabs

2 large onions (finely sliced lengthwise)
Salt $^1/_2$ tsp
Fresh mint leaves cleaned, washed and finely chopped
Green chillies 2-3 (finely chopped)
Fresh lemon juice $1^1/_2$ tbsp

Method

- Roast the poppy seeds, anis seeds, caraway seeds, brown cardamom seeds on a griddle on medium heat.
- Grind to a powder and mix with curd along with the red chilli powder, *garam masala* and the ginger-garlic paste.
- Mix the *masala* and the cornflour to the mince with 2 tbsp of water and knead for 5 minutes. Then mix the finely chopped coriander leaves.
- Divide the mince into 15-20 parts and flatten them. With a moist hand fold it on to skewer. Press the mince all around the skewer with moist fingers till it completely encircles it.
- Leave the skewers for about 20 minutes.
- The taste is more authentic if you roast on medium charcoal fire, turning slowly when one side is done and brushing with oil. Then turn the other side till it is fully done. The above process can be followed on the electric grill in an oven.
- Serve hot, cut into small pieces with the salad or with mint and coriander chutney.

Rogan Josh

Ingredients

Mutton 500 (medium sized pieces)
Curd 200 gms
Coriander seeds $^1/_2$ tbsp (ground)
Ginger 15 gms (shredded)
Pure *ghee* 2 tbsp
A pinch of asafoetida
Red chilli powder $^1/_4$ tsp
Kashmiri *garam masala* $^1/_4$ tsp
Dried ginger (*sonth* powder) $^3/_4$ tsp
Coriander leaves a few sprigs
Salt to taste
Water 200 ml for gravy

Method

- Mix the *ghee*, curd, asafoetida, salt, *sonth* and the mutton pieces thoroughly.
- Put them in a heavy-bottomed pan. Cook on medium heat till the whole liquid dries up and the *masala* starts sticking to the bottom of the pan.
- Add about 20 ml of water and continue cooking on medium heat.
- Repeat the second step thrice.

- Remove the pan from the fire and add the red chilli powder; stir well.
- Add 200 ml water and simmer on low heat, covering the pan with a tight lid. Cook till the meat is tender.
- When the meat is tender, take down the pan and add the Kashmiri *garam masala*, ground coriander seeds, shredded ginger and coriander leaves.
- Either put the dish in an oven on 250°F for about 25-30 minutes or put some live coals on the lid of the pan and put the pan on hot ash for about 30 to 40 minutes.
- Serve hot with *chappatis*.

Shabh Degh

Ingredients

Mutton 500 gms
Turnips 250 gms
Onion 1 large (thinly sliced)
Curd 200 gms (fresh, beaten)
Brown cardamom 3-4 (crushed)
Cinnamon 1"
Cloves 3-4
Sugar 1 tsp
Ginger 1" ground to a paste
Garlic 6-8 cloves
Coriander 2 tsp (ground coarsely)
Red chilli powder 1 tsp
Ghee or mustard oil 4 tbsp

Method

- Heat oil or *ghee* and fry the sliced onions till they are brown. Remove from pan. When cool, crush into powder.
- Fry the turnips and the meat separately till they are brown and remove from the oil/ *ghee*.
- In the same oil, add the cloves, brown cardamom and cinnamon. Fry till it gives a good fragrance.

- Add the ground *masala* of onion, garlic, ginger.
- Add the meat, turnip, crushed onion and salt to taste. Mix well and fry for 4-5 minutes, adding the chilli powder and coriander leaves.
- Now add the curd and about 3-4 *katoris* water. Cook on medium heat till the meat is tender and half the gravy remains. Serve with *chappati* or *nan*.

Glossary

SPICES

English	Hindi
Anis seed	Saunf
Asafoetida	Hing
Black cumin seeds	Kala jeera
Bay leaf	Tej patta
Basil	Kali tulsi
Cloves	Lavang or Laung
Cardamom (green)	Elaichi (Hari)
Brown cardamom	Moti/Badi Elaichi
Caraway seeds	Shah jeera
Cinnamon	Dalchini
Coriander seeds	Dhaniya (dry whole)
Cumin seeds	Jeera
Red chilli powder	Degi mirch
Fenugreek seeds	Methi seeds
Jaggery	Gur
Mango powder (raw/dried)	Amchoor
Mustard seeds	Sarson or rai
Pepper corns	Kali mirch (whole)
Poppy seeds	Khus khus
Pomegranate seeds	Anardana
Salt	Namak
Saffron	Kesar
Turmeric	Turmeric powder
Tamarind	Imli

All spices mixed	Garam masala

Note: *Garam masala* is a mixture of cinnamon, cloves, pepper corns, brown cardamoms and black cumin seeds. Some people also add a pinch of nutmeg and mace.

To make 100 gms *garam masala*:
30 gms black cardamom seeds
30 gms pepper corns
20 gms cinnamon
10 gms cloves (with flower from the head removed)
10 gms black cumin seeds.
Grind to a powder and pass through a sieve.
For Kashmiri *garam masala*, in addition to the above ingredients, add 4 blades mace (*javitri*) and about $^{1}/_{4}$ of nutmeg (*jaiphal*).

VEGETABLES

English	**Hindi**
Broad beans	Makhan beans
Beetroot	Chukandar
Bitter gourd	Karela
Calocassia	Arbi
Carrot	Gajar
Cabbage	Bandh gobhi
Cauliflower	Phul gobhi

Capsicum	Shimla mirch
Fenugreek leaves	Methi (Hari)
Ginger	Adrak
Garlic	Lehsan
Knol knol	Gath gobhi
Lemon	Nimbu
Mushroom	Khumb
Mint leaves	Pudina
Onion	Pyaz
Green onion (spring onions)	Hara pyaz
Green peas	Matar
Potatoes	Aloo
Pumpkin	Kaddu
Radish	Mooli
Spinach	Palak
Turnip	Shalgam
Lotus roots	Bhein or Nadru (in Kashmiri)
Tomatoes	Tamatar
Calocassia leaves	Arbi patte

DRY FRUITS

English	**Hindi**
Almond	Badam
Chestnut	Chilgoza
Coconut	Narial
Groundnut & Peanut	Moongphali

Cashewnut	Kaju
Raisins	Kishmish
Walnuts	Akhrot

MISCELLANEOUS

English	Hindi
Bengal gram	Kala chana
Broken gram	Chane ki dal
Whole black gram	Urad dal (whole)
Broken black gram	Urad dal chhilka (split)
Washed black gram	Urad dal dhuli
Large white gram	Kabuli chana
Refined flour	Maida
Rice	Chawal
Semolina	Sooji
Curd (yoghurt)	Dahi
Cream	Malai
Cottage cheese or Indian cream cheese	Paneer or chaman (in Kashmiri)
Gram flour	Besan
Wheat flour	Atta